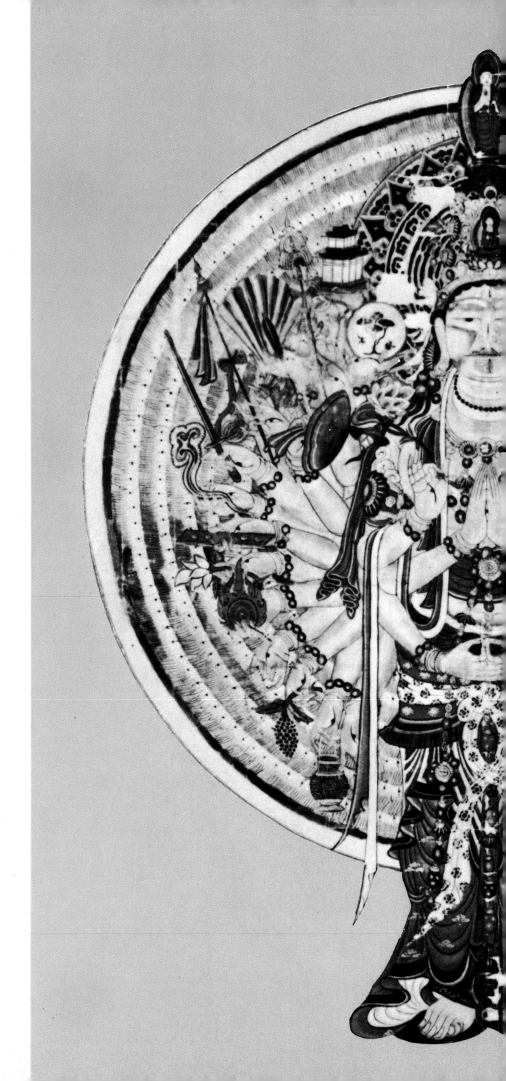

PORTRAITS OF GREATNESS

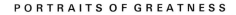

General Editor
ENZO ORLANDI

Text by
GABRIELE MANDEL SUGANA

Translated by
VIVIAN HART

Published by
The Hamlyn Publishing Group Ltd
London . New York . Sydney . Toronto
Hamlyn House, The Centre,
Feltham, Middlesex
© 1967 Arnoldo Mondadori Editore
Translation © 1968 by
The Hamlyn Publishing Group Ltd
Printed in Italy by
Arnoldo Mondadori, Verona

THE LIFE
AND
TIMES OF
BUDDHA

PAUL HAMLYN
London · New York · Sydney · Toronto

Below: Ancient place in the district of Amritsar, where about 5,000 years ago the ritual Vedic fire was lit. It has remained a sacred place in Brahmin and Hindu tradition, as a shrine to Agni, god of fire. The place has apparently not changed since prehistoric times.
Bottom left: in Benares, the

Jantar Mantar astronomical observatory. In India, many great astronomical buildings emerged in each era.
Right: reverse of 4th-century Sassanian coin, depicting a fire altar. The ancient worshippers of fire, followers of Zoroaster, still survive today in India under the name of Parsees.

AT THE FRONTIERS OF THE UNIVERSE

Let us look around for a moment and consider our environment. Do we not marvel at so much knowledge and technical progress, so many inventions? When we reflect how extensively the face of the world, and our own lives, have been changed by European civilization, we feel amazement and admiration. We have a civilization whose aim is the material welfare of man; and yet is seems to take on an increasingly turbulent character, so that eventually he who receives benefits from it becomes at the same time its prisoner. Man is no longer capable of appreciating a beautiful dawn or the simple joys of nature, and he loses contact with everything around him that is spiritual and not mechanical. Is there anywhere, outside a religious environment, where refuge may be found from the stresses of the modern world? Can we, at will, free ourselves from our obligations? Above all, is there anywhere we can escape to in order to find ourselves again? If we wish to discover antithesis to our material civilization, where self can merge with nature, where spiritual well-being is considered the ultimate aim, where an individual can free himself and can attain, or seem to attain, earthly happiness in a state of absolute serenity without regard for material welfare, this antithesis is in India; it is India. Here, in a sub-continent one third the size of Europe but seeming vast to us, great civilizations, magnificent empires, ideological and scientific developments have all left their influences; even though, in the ultimate analysis, we are left with the impression that life there has remained quite unchanged. Profound religious and philosophical ideas have evolved, that are in complete contrast to the analytical positivism of western culture. It is an extraordinary country: fire is still worshipped just as it was 5,000 years ago, and the land is cultivated by methods from the same period; amongst at least half the population life today is little different from that of 3,000 years ago; phenomena that Western science and medicine declare to be impossible actually happen every day. Since the beginning of time India has been a country which has had important cultural and commercial exchanges with the peoples of Mesopotamia, Egypt, Greece and Rome: yet in spite of this it belongs in our thoughts to the outer areas of mystery and the unattainable.

4

Left: An Indian country scene in the Agra district. Everyday life is still carried on as it was 3,000 years ago. Neither electricity nor the radio have yet reached it. The main highways that cross India have only one asphalted carriageway with a single earth track along the edges.
Below: In Benares, a pilgrim worships at an ancient sacred place: at a primitive sacred tree, but to new Hindu gods. Notwithstanding his appearance, he is an important University personality. In India today, clothing is often a simple loin-cloth. Women generally wear a long piece of seamless material, the sari.

FROM ZERO TO INFINITY

We are indebted to India for some of our most important astronomical knowledge; for the idea of the atom, conceived more than two thousand years ago; and for the first speculative notions that formed the basis of Hellenic philosophy. From her come Algebra and Arithmetic, as well as that cipher which, like India herself, represents the lowest and the greatest of all things: the zero. It was the Arabs who provided the bridge by which these disciplines reached the West. Musical notation and its terminology originated in India, where the first treatise on musical theory was written more than 2,000 years ago (the "Natya Sastra" of the 4th century B.C.). Likewise the first treatise on the art of government appeared in India (the "Arta Sastra" by Chanakya in the 3rd century). But India does not boast about these things: a civilization is born, passes away, and rises again as part of the eternal flux of life. For this reason,

the Indians have not thought it necessary to hand down to us an "historical" account of their origins. Nor is it improbable that iron was first discovered in the Ganges Valley, whence knowledge of it spread throughout the world. Certainly metal was founded in the Deccan region in very early historic times, and the exceptional quality of the ancient steel objects made on the subcontinent during this distant period, of which the column in Delhi is the most obvious example, still amazes experts today. The precise historical period of this ancient civilization, believed to be called Dravidian, is not yet known. What is known, however, is that a race evolved, rising apparently out of oblivion, which lived about 5,000 years ago in the Punjab and the Sindh, where they built Harappa and Mohenjo-Daro, where during recent excavations, buildings were discovered which proved the existence of a highly developed urban culture.

Above left: A small representation of a cart drawn by buffalo, recovered at Mohenjo-Daro. Terracotta of the Third millennium B.C., Indus Valley civilization (Karachi Museum).
Below: One of the most ancient "high places" in India. A stairway dug out of rock leads to the esplanade in Harappa where sacrifices were carried out. The "high places", which are known from India to Israel, were the points of contact with the Almighty.

Left: A drinking patera of carved stone, found at Harappa. It represents a man at a banquet sitting in the attitude typical of the Greeks and Romans. Indus Valley civilization.
Above: A miniature from Orissa representing Vishnu fighting Sahasrajuna. The episode reconstructs the fight between Rama and Ravana, told in the Ramayana, a 27,000 stanza epic poem (about 4th century B.C.), which recounts the Aryan conquests of South-East India.

THE CASTE SYSTEM

Below, left: The incarnation
(avatar) of Vishnu, a Hindu
miniature; right: a stone sculpture
in the sanctuary at Bubaneswara,
depicting the Hindu goddess Kali;
centre: another miniature depicting
"the whipping up of the Ocean",
one of the most important acts in
Hindu mythology.
Bottom left: The black Temple

of Konarak, near Puri, dedicated
to Surya, the sun-god. It is built
in the form of a square with
horses and wheels sculptured in
stone (13th century A.D.).
Bottom right: Interior of the temple
of Durga in Benares, called the
Temple of the Monkeys, with the
chapel where a very ancient statue
of the goddess Kali is worshipped.

Alongside the discoveries of ancient, highly organized cities, other archaeological excavations have uncovered cumuli of ashes and skeletons. They bear testimony to the violent way in which the Aryans, another branch of this migratory wave, descended into Persia: there are marked similarities in the beliefs of both ancient Persia and Vedic India. By 1000 B.C., the Aryans had created an empire in the Ganges plain; then, in successive waves, they invaded the rest of the peninsula. Relatively few in number, they were an authoritarian and individualistic people. In order to reign over the large Indian populace, they adopted the "caste system": the priest caste of the "brahmin", the warrior caste of the "kshatriya", the "vaishya" caste for workmen and native traders, and the "sudra" caste for the other conquered peoples. The caste system was sanctioned by the "Veda", the sacred books of Aryan culture. The Veda was composed between 1500 and 1300 B.C. and contains four books (Rig, Atharva, Sama, and Yajur-Veda). The vedic religion was originally a simple sacrificial ritual in which man sought to obtain favours from the gods of the Universe; but by degrees it was exalted into a formula of a more universal application. This had the effect of elevating the Brahmin who officiated at it to a position of absolute authority. The formula ("Brahman") became not only the key which was indispensable in order to pass to the life beyond, but also the force to which men in their material world, and the gods in their immaterial worlds, deferred. An individual soul of like substance can be identified in the "Atman" (self).

Left: Illustration from the "Rig
Veda", representing a divinity in
the clothing of a "kshatiya". The
Veda was composed between 1500
and 1300 B.C., and its four books
(Rig, Atharva, Sama and Yajur-
Veda) contain some of the most
ancient religious texts in the world,
being the religious and scientific
thought of the Brahmins. According
to legend, they were written
by the mythical Vyasa.

THE TWILIGHT OF THE GODS

The Brahman theology is contained in two texts, the "Brahmanas" and the "Upanishads". In them one reads: "The soul of all creatures is one soul, but it is also present in each creature; unity and plurality at the same time, like the reflection of the moon on water." This idea of individual dualism (body and soul) and of one universal spirit (man and cosmos) was also understood by the conquered peoples, since it supported their own belief in Samsara or metempsychosis. By desiring everlasting life for the individual, the lower classes could hope to be reborn into a higher body. The idea was developed in the doctrine of Karma (from "kar": act), which taught that rebirth was governed by acts accomplished during the present and all previous existences: "According to the acts achieved by man, so will his future existence be ordered," say the Upanishads. Karma offered various explanations: King Milinda asked the Buddhist sage Nagasena: "Why are men not all alike? Why do some have long life, some short, some health or illness, beauty or ugliness, courage or cowardice?" And the latter replied: "Why do not all plants resemble each other? Why, according to their species, are they sour or salty, bitter or acid, astringent or sweet?" "Because of the difference in their seeds," replied the King. "So do men differ according to the diversity of their acts which, like seeds of themselves, they have planted in former lives." But by the 7th century the two different conceptions had led to a turning away from the idea of continual rebirth. A convincing solution was sought; eventually the Brahmins put forward the theory of "full knowledge of the Atman Brahman", that is to say, the overcoming of self in order to identify oneself with the Universe and become as nothing within it. But a teacher was needed to explain the system and make it work. At this period numerous trends of thought developed which tried to escape from the inevitable fate of eternal rebirth, and which had equally in mind a reduction in the Brahmins' power. From an original seven theories and subdivisions of thought, in the 6th century there grew up about 60 creeds which sought to depose Brahmanism; and at the same time, the nobility caste tried to oust the Brahmins. Two main anti-Brahmin doctrines emerged from the khastriya caste: the Sankhya and Jainism.

Opposite page: Rani Vama with the newly-born deliverer Parasvanatha, Jain miniature (Victoria and Albert Museum, London). The Jains believe that Jina Mahavira, founder of their religion, had been preceded on earth by 23 other deliverers, the last of whom was the mythical Parasvanatha.

Top: Santanath and Adinath, saviours in the Jain pantheon, and Mahavira meditating; rock sculptures at Gwalior, in Madhya Pradesh (15th century).
Centre: The Jain temple at Sarnath, near the archaeological excavations which brought to light the Buddhist monasteries of the 4th century B.C.
Below: Jain sculptures on the right-hand wall of the gorge rising near the Fort of Gwalior (15th century). The Jain religion was founded by Vardhamana, a kshatriya born about 599 B.C. at Vaisali. His parents belonged to a sect who considered that birth is suffering and suicide a privilege. When Vardhamana reached the age of thirty, they let themselves die. He then gave up all wordly possessions and wandered through the Ganges valley preaching non-violence. He was called Jina Mahavira (Victorious Great Hero).

11

Right: Maya, wife of Suddhodana, chief of the Sakya, in a dream sees an elephant penetrating her right side; Gandhara stone sculpture (Central Museum, Lahore).
Below: The birth of the Buddha: Gandhara sculpture in green schist, (National Museum, Karachi). Gandhara art flourished between the 1st and 5th centuries in Afghanistan and Northern India under the Scytho-Iranian empire of the Kushana. It was an off-shoot of Greco-Roman art and of the Buddhist religion, and provided the first images of Siddhartha Gautama, who until then had been represented by abstract symbols.

A PRINCE IS BORN

Sankhya means number: by enumerating all the elements that make up a given piece of knowledge, or fact, or thing, one arrives at its metaphysical proof, that is to say, the ultimate essence of that knowledge, or fact, or thing. Not Atman, therefore, nor Brahman, but two firm principles: matter and spirit. The body is matter, and the spirit the breath of life. Without any intervention from the gods, and therefore from the Brahmins, man can – if he imposes the right actions on himself – subjugate Karma, weaken his own matter and succeed in liberating himself even when he is still living. The way is by meditation, mystical practice, "yoga". Modern Theosophy and the Anthroposophy of Rudolf Steiner were derived from the Sankhya, but in Europe it is its more spectacular side that is especially well-known: the "sadhu" who lives in a state of meditation, pierces himself with nails and knives, and assumes forced postures for years on end. In India today, ascetics, of whatever caste they may be, still form a company of venerated and powerful saintly men. Jainism was founded by the nobleman Mahavira, a contemporary of the Buddha. He preached the supremacy of inevitable fate, and the liberation of self by conquering Karma by non-violent methods. Since actions motivated by desire are like toxins that accumulate in the body and poison it, it is better to destroy the desire. In the same way it is better to be seated than standing, lying down than seated, asleep than lying down, dead than asleep. Mahavira, proclaimed Jina (conqueror, hence Jainism), had, like the Buddha, spiritual predecessors and many temporal followers; and in India today there are a million and a half faithful. Mahatma Gandhi was a Jain who, in the struggle for Indian independence, transferred the theory of non-violence to the political sphere. At the furthest limits of this multi-racial land, to the North-East of the state of Kosala, there flourished in the 6th century B.C. the confederation of the Sakya. Here the influence of the Aryan invaders penetrated gently, like the last wave of the sea on the sand, and its distance from the main centres weakened the ascendancy of the Brahmins. Here Siddhartha Gautama was born to Suddhodana Gautama, chief of the Sakya, and his wife, Maya, in the "vaisaka" month somewhere between 563 and 556 B.C.

Top: Siddhartha Gautama carries off a prize in archery, showing extraordinary skill; painting in the grotto Temple at Dambulla (Matala, Ceylon).
Above left: The Buddha's birth in Lumbini Park; 18th-century Tibetan painting (Guimet Museum, Paris).
Right: Siddhartha's bath. The gods Indra and Brahma are pouring

water on the infant. Gandhara high-relief (National Museum, Peshawar). According to the canonical texts, miraculous events took place at the birth and during the infancy of the future Buddha. By a display of superhuman skill, Siddhartha was able to overwhelm his adversaries and win for himself the cousin whom he wished to marry.

A GOLDEN CHILDHOOD

Numerous legends have overlaid the birth of the Buddha with symbolism and miraculous events. Buddhists themselves recognize two ways of looking at the life of their founder, with their eyes and with their heart. The heart accepts all the legends, the miracles, the deification; while the eyes believe only what they see, that which is capable of irrefutable proof. But the historical image of the Buddha has been gradually worn away under a weight of legend. It is not known, for example, if Maya's premonitory vision is symbolic or an historical fact. According to the story, Maya, having lived for the 32 months of her marriage in a state of total asceticism and being on that account still a virgin, dreamed that an elephant pierced her side. Ten months later, in Lumbini Park, a son was born to her, coming out of her side while she stood holding on to the branches of a fig-tree. There is no doubt, however, as to the legendary background of the seven steps that the new-born infant was supposed to have immediately taken towards the four cardinal points, and from whose steps lotus flowers, the symbol of purity, blossomed; nor of the words he was supposed to have uttered. But his presentation at the temple of the god, Abhaya, is according to the custom of that time. Here the Brahmins found on his body the 32 large marks and the 80 smaller marks of a "great man", and the sage Asita prophesied that, according to his own choice, he would become either a powerful emperor or an ascetic who would deliver man from the evils of the world. Seven days after his birth his mother died, after giving the baby into the care of her sister Mahapajati, Suddhodana's second wife. Suddhodana himself was greatly impressed by Asita's prophecy, and he had Siddhartha brought up within the confined area of the palace walls and the park, so that he might know nothing of the world's ills. Thus the boy grew up amidst laughter and singing and knew many happy days, sheltered from all suffering and misery. Yet he was not idle or thoughtless in this time; for he studied, and read, and took part in competitions and duels, in which he showed great skill. At the age of 16, he fell in love with Gopa Yasodhana and married her after beating her other suitors in several trials of physical and intellectual prowess including an archery contest of the utmost severity.

Opposite, above: Dancers and musicians making merry during festivities at court; Gandhara stone relief.
Below: Siddhartha Gautama's four encounters, with an old man, a sick person, a funeral, and a beggar-monk; 11th-century relief in gilded terracotta (Pagan Temple, Burma).
This page, left: A lady amusing herself at court; 19th-century miniature, Punjab (Victoria and Albert Museum, London).
Above, left: Siddhartha between three concubines; 2nd-century sculpture of Amaravati origin (British Museum, London).
Right: A palace festivity, 1st-century sculpture in the Queen's Grotto at Udaygiri.
Below: A Brahmin blesses the king and the court festivities; Hindu miniature in Malwa (W. G. Archer Collection, London).
Hindu courts preferred singing and dancing of a highly sensual character, appropriate to the Indian artistic temperament, rather than riches and pomp.

THE PRINCE FINDS HIS DESTINY

The years passed pleasantly in the three palaces and four gardens that Suddhodana gave his son. But one day, while making his way from one garden to another in his golden chariot, driven by Channa, his charioteer, the prince wished to vary his route, and on the way he met an old man of 80 struggling along under the burden of his infirmity. "Why is that man suffering?" Siddhartha asked the charioteer, and he replied: "This is life, my lord". Siddhartha went out a second time and met a man groaning in pain. Another day, he saw a funeral procession, and was greatly saddened by the tears and grief of the relatives accompanying the dead man. Finally, a fourth time, he met an ascetic peacefully begging as he went along, wearing ragged clothes but with a serene expression on his face. He then understood what was his destiny, and hastened back to the palace where the birth of his son, Rahula, was being celebrated. That night, while his guests and concubines and dancing girls lay sleeping in disarray, Siddhartha wandered among them deep in thought, contemplating the vanity of earthly pleasures. He then woke his father, and asked his permission to seek shelter with the Masters of the Sankhya. He said goodbye to his sleeping wife and son, saddled his horse and, accompanied by the faithful Channa, made his way to the forest. There he dismounted and cut off his long hair with his sword, which he then gave to the charioteer. Then he sent him away, and after exchanging his fine clothing for a beggar's rags, he started walking South, full of a sense of peace and exaltation. Thus, on the night of his 29th birthday, Siddhartha embarked upon his chosen course.

Opposite: Siddhartha Gautama leaves the palace on the night of his 29th birthday; painting in the Grotto Temple at Dambulla (Matala, Ceylon). Above, left: Siddhartha cuts off his hair with his sword; 11th-century terracotta bas-relief (Pagan Temple, Burma). Right: The remains of Siddhartha's palace at Kapilavastu. Only a few stones are left of the magnificent dwellings, which are still visited and revered by the faithful, and they are only remembered by historians because the Buddha once lived there. Archaeologists have been able to locate the remains of the palaces where the Buddha lived, and the monasteries where the early monks met, with the help of ancient descriptions left by Chinese pilgrims.
Right, below: Siddhartha cuts off his hair; 17th-century Tibetan painting (Guimet Museum, Paris).

THE RETREAT AT URUVILVA

Below, left: The forest at Uruvilva (or Uruvela) near Gaya, in the state of Bihar, where Siddhartha Gautama meditated. Right: Sujata offers Siddhartha a cup of rice cooked in sweetened milk as refreshment. This is one of the 1,100 8th-century stone reliefs that decorate the Temple of Borobodur in Java.

Gautama became a pilgrim wandering in search of truth. First of all he became the disciple of the nobleman Alara Kalama, who taught him yogic meditation leading to the state known as "the sphere of nothingness". But Siddhartha was still dissatisfied, and leaving this master he made his way to another great teacher, Uddaka Ramaputta, who practised in the Pandava mountains near Rajaghra, capital of the Magadha region. Uddaka Ramaputta taught Gautama to reach an even higher state of concentration. He quickly attained this, but realized that this too was not the final goal he sought. For this reason he left Magadha as well, and with five companions who admired his thirst for perfection he withdrew to the Forest of Uruvilva, near Gaya, in the state of Bihar. His sojourn on the banks of the Nairanjana lasted six long years, during which time the key to his daily existence was abstinence and ascetic practice. Sometimes he ate only a single grain of rice a day; sometimes he remained standing on his feet for weeks on end, weakening the flesh in order to move the spirit. To illustrate more vividly the earthly temptations, the difficulties of meditation, and

the victory that an altruistic soul must try to win by mortifying itself for the good of others, legend has it that Mara, god of sensual pleasures, came down to earth in order to test Gautama's resolution, and hurled against him rain, lightning, and violent winds. But in vain; for nothing could divert him from his chosen course. After a while, however, Gautama recognized the vanity of mortification, which seemed to him now to be no less ambitious in itself than the thirst for power. Accordingly he devoted himself to the path of the "middle way", rejecting all extremism on the ground that it was in the final analysis more harmful than beneficial. One day a woman called Sujata, who happened to be passing by on her way to a sacred tree, offered him a cup of milk-rice that she was carrying as a dedication to that tree. Gautama accepted the refreshment. Then, donning a shroud offered him by a dying female slave, he bathed himself in the river. His five companions observed him and it seemed to them that by his actions Gautama appeared to have renounced asceticism. They left him in disgust and set off on foot for Benares.

Above: Miniature from Orissa, depicting Siddhartha Gautama meditating and being worshipped by two Brahmin divinities. He is holding a rosary in his hand, a typical sacred and magic amulet of the early Buddhist monks, which later passed into other religions. Left: Two ascetics in the forest; a guru (master) is teaching a pupil. The background of the miniature, painted in bright red, indicates the urgency and passion of truth; illustration by Markendeya Purana (about 1785), Punjab (W. G. Archer Collection, London). Indian ascetics (called sadhu or, incorrectly, yogi or fakirs) are divided into nine sects, and enjoy the privileges and veneration that Christians normally reserve for saints.

19

Below: Mara, richly dressed as "lord of the upper sky", on the back of an elephant; fresco in the Temple of Telvatta (Galle, Ceylon). Mara is considered by Buddhists to be the mortal god of material things in heaven as well as in hell. His three daughters – Voluptuousness, Lust and Anxiety – are all equally transient. Right: Two representa- tions of the Buddha meditating – assailed by Mara's demons (7th-century fresco, Ajanta Grottoes); and during his first period of meditation, when he remembers being taken by his father into the countryside and feeling pity for the peasants. He appears adorned in jewels of a Sakya prince (Gandhara relief, Peshawar Museum).

CONDEMNED TO LIVE AN EARTHLY LIFE

A Gandhara high-relief: Mara's demon army prepares to fight Siddhartha Gautama as he is deep in meditation. "Mara's Temptation" is one of the most widely represented events in the Buddha's life, because it offers such a choice of imagery with its many fantastic demons, and because it has a direct connection with daily life in which man is constantly assailed by the temptations of fleeting earthly pleasures. We even find the fearful masks of the Gandharan demons in Romanesque and Gothic sculptures in France. It is probable that the paintings which were traded along the Silken Way provided a common inspiration.

It was the day of his 35th birthday. He spent the afternoon resting in a small wood. At dusk, he started off towards Gaya. When he met a Brahmin collecting grass for a sacrifice, he asked him for eight sheaves, and with them he made for himself a grass mat under a tree. He walked round the trunk seven times, then sat upon the mat, murmuring: "Let my skin wither, my hands grow numb, my bones dissolve; until I have attained understanding I will not rise from here." He placed his tongue on his palate and his right hand on the ground, and entered into meditation. The hosts of Mara, the Evil One, approached and claimed the throne of grass which he had made for himself. Gautama touched earth, calling the earth to witness that the throne was his by right, and the earth gave witness. He spent the first watch of the night contemplating his former lives, drawing forth memories of them from his subconscious mind. In the second watch of the night he developed the "divine eye", and before his mental vision there appeared myriads of beings, ceaselessly coming to be and passing away: men and animals, bright gods from the highest heavens, spirits from the lower realms. Some had long and blissful lives, others short and painful, and each, in strict accordance with the deeds done in one existence, went on to a further life of weal or woe, and yet another, ceaselessly. Even the mightiest gods were not exempt from change but, like all other beings, were enmeshed in the net of Karma, condemned to fare on endlessly in the cycle of becoming, like an everlasting sentence to life, for passion bound them all. In the third vigil he became aware of the transcending of all passions, and knew that he had achieved this. He saw clearly the nature of things as they truly are, and thus was the fully Enlightened One, the Buddha. Buddha means "Awakened", and he was now like a man who had been dreaming and was now fully awake. He understood that consciousness is the result of ignorant modes of awareness, ever-repeated from the beginningless past, binding man by fond desires to the wheel of rebirth. But now freedom from this state had been won. Nirvana, the Deathless, had been gained. For he knew that "Destroyed is birth, perfected is the ascetic life, that which had to be done is done. There is no more rebirth for me."

BUDDHA: THE ENLIGHTENED ONE

Truth had become clear to him in a series of dazzling revelations: "How unhappy this world is! One grows old and dies only to be born again, to grow old and to die yet again, in an endless cycle. Birth and the desire for birth is the cause of this misery. If one could kill the desire that leads from birth to birth, new rebirths and new suffering could be prevented. There is only one way to extinguish desire: to realize its true nature." Gautama had entered into the supraconscious, a state of existence that is both individual and universal, and extends at the same moment of time over the past and the future, linking the single mind to the infinite universe. He had been "awakened" to the true life, he was the Enlightened One, the Buddha. He then spent the next four weeks thinking about the Cosmos, without rising from his mat. Mara, the god of sensual pleasure, tried to bring him back to earthly materialism, sending him his three most beautiful daughters, Lust, Anxiety and Voluptuousness; but their beautiful, vain appearance was wasted on the pure eyes of the Enlightened One. The King of the Underworld and of Material Things then snatched away the grass mat that the Buddha had made for himself. He tried to turn him from his resolve by pointing out the terrifying immensity of the task that awaited him, and the difficulty of explaining his newly-acquired wisdom to a multitude of men blinded by ignorance, suspicion and hate. Worse still, this new knowledge might encourage man to further acts of injustice and ambition. The saintly ascetic was sorely beset by doubt. But with the help of infinite mercy he was able to overcome this ultimate test, and once again he touched the earth with his right hand, so that it might bear witness. Legend tells that the Earth appeared and routed Mara and his demons. Then the Buddha burst into a Song of Victory: "Many dwellings in life have imprisoned me and I constantly sought the builder of this prison of my senses, which suffering made real. My struggle was frantic, but now I know the builder of this tabernacle. Never more will he build these walls of suffering, nor erect the architrave of falsehood, nor place new beams in the clay. The dwelling is crumbling and the architrave breaks, because now I know the name of the builder: it is Illusion!" And the Buddha rose and set off towards Benares.

Left, and opposite: Frescoes from Central Asia, representing heavenly festivities. According to Buddhist legends, when Siddhartha received enlightenment 7,000 heavens rejoiced, and angels and archangels wept for joy (Museum of Chinese Art, Parma).
Below: The Tree of Enlightenment at whose foot

Siddhartha became the Buddha. The original tree which was worshipped at Bodh Gaya withered away in 1879, but one of its branches was transplanted and a new tree grew from it. Other branches have been transplanted to Ceylon and Sarnath. At 2,500 years old it is the oldest continuously documented tree in the world.

23

INDIA DISCOVERS MAN

Left: The gesture of charity and of teaching in a Chinese statue of the Avalokitesvara Buddha (of helpful benevolence). Gilded plaster, Yuan dynasty, (1280–1367).
Below: An ascetic's retreat in the forest of Kapilavastu. Here the Buddha stripped himself of all his possessions in order to try and give knowledge to his fellow men.

When he left Bodh Gaya, where he had gained enlightenment, the Buddha began a long period, lasting 45 years, during which he taught his followers a new world of truth, life and example. From that moment he travelled around, preaching continuously; he attracted to him men longing for peace; he accomplished many miracles, and taught his word in eloquent speeches, by example and by meaningful periods of silence; he came into contact with many earthly events—fighting, wars, rivalries—without being corrupted by them. Above all he repeatedly declared that he was neither a divine being nor a divinity, but one of those "sent" who, at each of the earth's cosmic evolutions, come down to enlighten man. It is impossible to reconstruct the itinerary of his various missions; for in order to be objective, history must disregard legend. It is equally difficult to sum up his teaching because, although it is so clear, simple and precise, it is also structurally frail, varied in argument, and highly elusive. But as he lay dying Buddha said in summary of his teaching, "In all the visible and invisible worlds there exists one single, equal power, without beginning or end, without any laws but its own, without preference or aversion. It kills and saves without any other aim than to carry out its Destiny. Death and Suffering are the shuttles of its loom; Love and Life are its children. But do not try to measure the Incommensurable with words, nor to plumb the depths of the Impenetrable with the rope of thought: it is wrong to question; it is wrong to reply. Expect nothing from the pitiless gods; for they too submit to the laws of the Karma, and are born, grow old and die to be reborn, without being able to free themselves from their own suffering. Do not forget that as each man creates for himself his own prison, so may he also acquire a power superior to that of the gods." The Buddha sharply attacked the general feeling of apathy in India, and undermined Brahmanism by the compelling nature of his theories. Brahmanism had developed the idea of the existence of the perceptible and of the apparent; but having accepted that suffering was inevitable, it had not considered the individual: everything was collective and collectivity was represented by the caste system. By specifying that the main cause of suffering was craving, and the cure, awareness of it, Gautama was the first to place an emphasis on the absolutely unique rights of "I". Through Buddhism, India discovered man.

*Above: Chinese jade sculpture, Ming era. It represents a fruit called the "hand of Buddha" because of its close resemblance to a hand held out in a typical gesture of charity if laid on its side, and of teaching if placed upright. Far left: The mouth of a monk's cell, sculptured in the shape of a tiger's head, where the Buddhists in Orissa used to retire to meditate. It is situated at the summit of Udaygiri hill.
Left: Avalokitesvara in adoration of the Bodhisattva Samantabhadra; an illustration from the Astasahasrika Prajnaparamita (Perfect Wisdom), which is 8,000 verses long (Victoria and Albert Museum, London).*

THE SERMON AT BENARES

Below: Gandhara sculpture depicting a Buddha with his right hand raised in the sign of protection; on his palm is engraved the Wheel of the Law. His left hand holds a jar of ambrosia. His hair is gathered into the "ushnisha" (a top-knot on the crown of the head). On his forehead he has the "urna" or "third eye").

The Buddha came to Benares and there he encountered the five companions who had earlier abandoned him. He said to them: "I am the Tathagata, the one who has come to teach you the Law, the Dharma." At first they were unwilling to hear him, but the nobility of his presence overcame their reluctance. After a while the Enlightened One continued: "Hear the noble truth concerning suffering. Birth is suffering; old age is suffering; as too is death; as too are being exposed to what one dislikes, separation from what one likes, and failure to realize one's desires. And this is the noble truth concerning the sources of suffering: they are the desire for sense-pleasures, the will-to-live, the will-to-die. And this is the noble truth concerning the suppression of suffering: it is the utter passionless giving up of craving and desire. And this is the way of the Eightfold Path that leads to the annihilation of suffering: it is the middle way between asceticism and worldly life; discovered by Tathagata, it unseals the eyes of the spirit, leads to peace of mind, to knowledge, to enlightenment, to Nirvana. The steps of the noble Eightfold Path are: Right Understanding, Right Resolve, Right Speech, Right Behaviour, Right Occupation, Right Effort, Right Mindfulness, and Right Concentration." Then the Buddha explained the reality of the "non-I" and the phenomenology of the "twelve linked causes": because of ignorance, there are habit-patterns; because of habit-patterns, there is consciousness; because of consciousness, there is mind-and-body; because of mind-and-body, there are the six senses; because of the six senses, there is touch; because of touch, there is sensation; because of sensation, there is craving; because of craving, there is grasping; because of grasping, there is individual existence; because of individual existence, there is repeated earthly existence; because of repeated earthly existence, there is decay and death. Finally the Buddha stated the three causes of suffering, the six states of transmigration, and the twelve stages of human existence. Then the companions elected to follow the Dharma; a young man of Benares was the first to utter the ritual formula of ordination: "I take refuge in the Buddha, I take refuge in the Dharma, I take refuge in the Sangha (the monastic community)."

Opposite page, above: At Sarnath (Benares), remains of the Buddhist monastery buildings in the hermitage of Mrgadava, or Deer Park. Here the Buddha converted the first five companions. In the park, many deer still freely graze today within the vast enclosures.
Below, left: A very ancient fire altar at Sarnath. Here, since time immemorial, Indians have come to worship the divine gods. Close by this altar, the Buddha gave his first sermon at Sarnath.
Below, right: Stupa built on the place where the Buddha held his first sermon and gained his first followers, known as the five companions.

THE GIFT OF THE BAMBOO GROVE

At the end of the rainy season, when the Buddha decided to go to Uruvilva, seventy monks followed him. On the way, he explained the Dharma to them with many parables, taking his inspiration from chance encounters and events to make comparisons and give examples. To one who asked him to explain cosmology, that he might know what substance the world was made of, so that he might save himself from it, he replied: "What is the use of knowing the theories concerning its composition? They will change with each new discovery. If you were struck by a poisoned arrow, would you want to know, before having it attended to, who drew the bow, from what tree the wood had been taken, what the horse was like with whose mane it was bound, what caste the archer belonged to, what colour were his clothes? Would you not hurry away instead before the poison started to work?" He admonished others thus: "My thoughts have travelled throughout the world, but I have never found anything more precious to man than his own "I". Since, for each one of us, our own self is the most important, respect the self of your fellow-man as you respect your own." To the multitudes, he advised: "Be compassionate, and respect even the lowest form of life; give and receive freely, but do not take by force; never lie, even on occasions when lying seems excusable; do not take drugs or alcohol; respect women and do not commit impure acts." In reply to a Brahmin who considered himself to be superior to all ascetics, he delivered the Sermon of Fire: "Everybody is inflamed by the fire of desire... and everything is only illusory flame that spends itself." One day, at Rajaghra, during a banquet that King Bimbisara was giving for the Buddhists, he accepted the gift of the Veluvana (Bamboo Grove) where he built a vihara (monastery). While the Buddha was present at the banquet, one of his new disciples, Assaji, met the ascetic Sariputra. The latter, impressed by the calm dignity of the novice, asked him who his master was, and what doctrine he preached. The reply that he made has remained one of the fundamental truths of Buddhism: "Of all that has an origin He has explained the ending. He who has explained things in this way is the Great Master."

Opposite page: Shah-jiki Dheri relief depicting a royal couple, perhaps King Bimbisara, or possibly Hariti and Panchika, two Brahman divinities that are also included in the Buddhist group of gods (Museum, Peshawar); a bod-hisattva on the path of enlighten-ment, fresco in the first grotto at Ajanta; Buddha in the attitude of protection, a Chinese sculpture of the T'ang era (618–907) clearly showing Greek influence. At that time, these small statues were placed in the temples when a favour was requested, and their heads and hands were later mutilated if the favour was not granted (Shih Ch'eng Collection, Formosa). This page: King Bimbisara giving the Buddha the Veluvana (Bamboo Grove) where a monastery (vihara) will be built. The Buddha raises his right hand in the sign of protection. A female disciple is coming forward from the left to give her rich diadem to the Order. The first five companions of the Enlightened One stand on his right. (Sikri sculpture, Central Museum, Lahore).

THE BUDDHA RETURNS TO HIS FATHER'S HOUSE

The time came when Gautama yielded at last to his father's many invitations, and decided to preach at Kapilavastu. The journey was slow, lasting two months, and Suddhodana was angry and did not go to meet his son when he finally arrived. Nor did the proud Sakya wish to bow their head to the Buddha. According to legend, the Buddha then raised himself off the ground and obliged his former companions to humble themselves before him. Then he went begging from door to door, and after a long sermon converted his father and the nobles. After their reunion, his wife sent their son, Rahula, to him to claim his share in his inheritance. The Buddha turned to one of his followers and said: "Receive him into the Order." In this way he converted 500 Sakya, amongst them his half-brother Nanda; but Nanda left him (the story is told in the Saundarananda-Kavya, one of the finest Buddhist works) for the love of the beautiful Janapadakalyani. Whereupon Siddhartha showed him a monkey which had been horribly mutilated in a forest fire; then he transported him in spirit to the court of the god Indra, where the beautiful Apsaras were dancing, so that he might see the difference between an earthly creature exposed to the evils of the world, and the beauty of the spirit freed from the illusions of the senses. Thus many of the Buddha's cousins were also con-

verted, among whom were Anuruddha, Mahanama, his favourite disciple, Ananda, who served the Master until his death, and Devadatta, who later betrayed him. When he left Kapilavastu, the Buddha returned to Rajagrha, where he converted Anathapindika, a merchant from Sravasti, who built resting places every mile between the two cities, and gave to the Order the Grove of Jetavana at Sravasti, purchasing it with as much gold as would have covered its entire area. The beautiful Vishaka obtained another monastery for the monks by giving them her magnificent diadem; and when the Buddha went to Vaisali, he accepted the invitation of the courtesan Amrapali, and it was she who provided the monks with a palace and a park. However bloody events befell the parents and friends of the Enlightened One. Before leaving Kapilavastu, the Buddha had prophesied a bloody fate for the Sakya and death by fire for the aggressor. After Suddhodana's death, these predictions were fulfilled. Prasenajit, King of Kosala, was deposed by his evil son, Virudhaka, who moved against the Sakya with a powerful army; he easily conquered them, since the Sakya declined to fight, in accordance with the Buddhist precept that "not-to-kill is the supreme law". Immediately afterwards, Virudhaka was himself burnt to death at his palace.

Below: One of the Buddha's miracles. The Japanese monk Zenmui has invoked his image, and is being rescued from cut-throats; 19th-century Japanese engraving of the Ukiyo-Ye School. This event is very similar to the assault on the Buddha by the brigand Angulimala; he was following the Enlightened One to kill him, but however fast he ran he was unable to overtake the Buddha. Right: The Buddha stops a furious elephant that the traitor Devadatta has set on him with the intention of killing him by infusing the animal with charitable love; this is a second or third-century relief of Amaravati origin (National Museum, Madras).

SEVENTY-SEVEN MIRACLES

Below: A Gandhara relief, representing one of the Buddha's miracles. He is shown subduing a terrible black serpent sent to kill him while he is staying in the hut of the ascetic Kasyapa. The Buddha's body is glowing so brightly that a monk runs up with a jar of water, thinking that the hut has caught fire (Central Museum, Lahore).

Bottom: A miniature depicting one of the Buddha's journeys in the heavens, as he flies over Hell and sees the terrible sufferings of the people there as they are tortured by demonic figures; illustration from the "Nimi Jataka", 19th-century example of Burmese art (Guimet Museum, Paris).

When all the prophecies made at Kapilavastu came true, the Buddha was asked why he had not wished to intervene by using his divine powers. He replied in this way, in the Sermon at Katigrama: "He who has a healthy mind does not compete with the world nor condemn it: meditation will teach him that nothing here below is lasting, except the troubles we undergo in life. Meditation will fill him with such light that the three passions of lust, anger and ignorance that darken the spirit will be extinguished, and he will enter into the way of salvation that leads beyond dominion over life and death; because his mind will no longer interest itself in earthly things, but will fix itself on the supreme good." He always advised his monks not to work miracles, emphasising that conversions should be the result of moral conviction only. When the monk Pindola flew three times over the heads of his rivals, the Enlightened One compared him to a prostitute who beautifies herself in order to obtain favours. However, many miracles—77 in all —are ascribed to the Buddha in the sacred texts. At Vaisali, and elsewhere he brought outbreaks of plague to an end; before King Prasenajit he multiplied his own image; he roused, or calmed, storms; and several times preached simultaneously in different places. Before going to Kapilavastu, he sent his childhood friend, Udayin, ahead of him through space, so that he might take the food that was to be offered to him there. Again, he made his monks cross the River Ganges in the air. One day, in the state of Kosala, he walked calmly through a forest where the brigand, Angulimala, ruled supreme; the latter, furious, followed him in order to kill him. But however fast he ran, he could not manage to catch up with the Buddha, who still walked peacefully before him. When at last he stopped exhausted, the Enlightened One turned to him and said: "However fast you run, you will never reach the extremity of space, which is the physical limit for those who do not have knowledge. Sit down and listen to the Dharma." On another occasion, the seven heretics at Sravasti, knowing that he had accomplished a miracle under a mango tree, destroyed all the mango trees in the region. But the Buddha took a mango and planted the seed of it, and a mango tree miraculously flowered.

BETRAYALS AND PERSECUTIONS

So the Buddha accomplished many miracles. One day he explained how the earth trembles, not only for physical causes such as earthquakes, but also at the moment of enlightenment when a saint touches the earth and calls on it to bear witness; and when cosmic energy influences its rotation; but above all, when a Buddha enters Nirvana, because then the earth itself trembles with excitement. A Buddha's energy, he said, "is extraordinarily powerful, sublime, of evident and incalculable effectiveness". Notwithstanding this, many sought to set themselves up in opposition to the considerable power of his word and his Dharma. The Brahmins undoubtedly appreciated the threat to the religious values upon which their own ascendancy had been established. But the most severe persecutions did not come from them. In the first place the Buddha, while not accepting their gods, did not altogether deny them. Secondly, the people as a whole were not greatly influenced by, or concerned with, teaching at such an exalted level. Rather, the danger came from his own followers and, in particular, from his cousin Devadatta. At first, Devadatta was his disciple. But he grew covetous of his power and sought to rouse the monks against him. By a display of some of the magic powers he had learnt, he persuaded Ajatasatru, son of King Bimbisara, to have his father put to death, so that he could ascend the throne of Magadha. He was successful in persuading the Vrji monks of Vaisali to break away, and they arrogantly assumed a rigorous form of ascetism, abandoning the more humane "middle way" of the Buddha. Devadatta then sought to kill the Buddha. First he sent hired assassins against him, but they fell blinded by a bright light as soon as they approached him. Next Devadatta tried to make a pillar fall on him, but it stopped miraculously in mid-air. Finally he drugged an elephant and sent him running along a walled pathway as the Buddha approached from the opposite direction. But the Enlightened One infused the virtue of charitable love into the great animal, so that the creature knelt down in adoration before him. At this point, so the legends tell, the dissident monks returned to the Order, and Devadatta repented and begged for pardon.

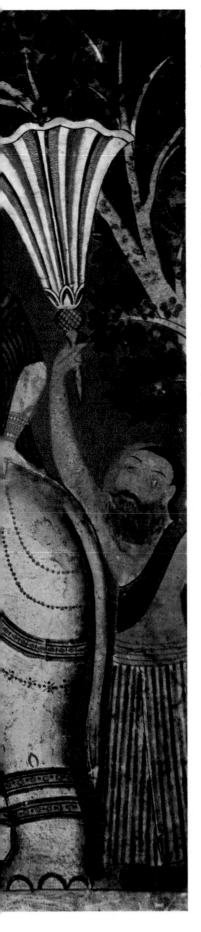

Left: A king on the back of an elephant, presumably an illustration of Ajatasatru's exploits or possibly of King Taxila; Pahala monastery, at Mulgirigala (Hambantota, Ceylon). These 18th-century frescoes keep alive the most ancient Buddhist traditions. Near left: Nanda, the Buddha's half-brother, Gandhara relief.

Above: An attempt by Devadatta, Buddha's cousin and jealous rival, on his life; some workmen are trying to drop a pillar on the Enlightened One, but he miraculously stops it in mid-air, and no one can move it again; Gandhara relief. Near left: The protective Buddha who saves others from disaster as well as himself; Chinese bronze of the Ming dynasty (1368–1643) (Museum of Chinese Art, Parma). Legends have considerably magnified the number of Devadatta's attempts on the Buddha's life, which also took place during their earlier lives.

ONE, NONE, OR A HUNDRED THOUSAND

The Buddha travelled through the Eastern part of the Ganges valley preaching, teaching and accomplishing miracles. When he had touched the ground with one hand at the moment of enlightenment, his mind had been uplifted beyond the limits of thought at that time, and in the same way his Dharma (which derived its origin from traditional Indian thought) projected itself into limitless new ways of thought. India, as we saw at the beginning, covers an immense territory: it flourishes and thrives without man's interference, and man is suffocated, as it were, under the oppressive canopy of monsoon clouds for eight months of the year. This conditions the spirit into a state of resigned acceptance, so that the native Indian, who is tied to tradition and to the earth, must perforce humble himself. India is so vast that it can contain contemplative and metaphysical sciences reaching the heights of abstraction and also nihilistic religions. Was it the Buddha's intention to propagate new scientific knowledge in the form most appropriate to his own times, as a speculative science? It seems probable, since he proclaimed that contemplation and asceticism were ends in themselves, and constantly preached the need for spiritual activity and the obligation on the part of the individual to seek for himself. But, for India, the only form of reality was thought; whereas matter is merely the tangible expression of that thought. This reality can only be revealed through the senses, but the senses —because they express and perceive inadequately— cannot provide consciousness with an exact image of the world. As Pirandello says, there can be one, none, or a hundred thousand ways of seeing. The Buddha created a physical science with the clay his own earth provided at that time. He was often in doubt as to how to carry out his mission, fearing that he might be misunderstood or that he might give men knowledge that was too difficult or too dangerous. He gave a clear solution to human destiny: our earthly life is conditioned by and composed of our body, our sensations, ideas, emotions and consciousness—all of which are transitory. This very impermanence of our nature permits metempsychosis, and when this is complete, Nirvana is finally attained.

Above: The Buddha seated beneath the Tree of Enlightenment. With his right hand he touches the ground and calls upon it to bear witness (relief in green schist). Left: A carved tympanum depicting episodes in the life of the Buddha and his deification. The conversion of the Naga prince Apalala, who was laying waste to the district of Swat; worship of the Buddha by earthly and heavenly bodies; and worship of his begging bowl (Peshawar Museum). The Buddha did not categorically deny the old beliefs and gods, but rather created a synthesis of current modes of thought. Until recently it was thought that he had taught an exclusively ethical and philosophical discipline; and his scientific teaching and his theories on physics have only been clarified and evaluated in the light of new discoveries. They form a mysterious and fantastic corollary to the main body of his teaching.

Below: Chinese bronze of the T'an dynasty (618–907) depicting the lotus flower which grows in purity out of its earthly elements (Museum of Chinese Art, Parma). The symbolic interpretations and superstitions which surround the Buddhist lotus are very numerous.
Right: Maitreya bodhisattva, an Afghan fresco in the grottoes at Bamiya (6th–7th century).
Far right: a tapestry representing a female Buddhist donor, discovered in the oasis at Kucha, Central Asia (Arts and Crafts Museum, Berlin). In the steppes region of Central Asia, many ancient remains of Buddhist art works have survived and are of great value to the collector.

EVERYTHING EXISTS, NOTHING EXISTS

A most revealing anecdote is told about the Buddhist sect of Zen: a pupil came to the master and asked what was Truth. The master replied: "Do you see that I am not holding a spade in my hand?" "I see that," replied the pupil. "Go and dig with it then!" was the reply. The Buddha has, in fact, set man at the crossroads of these two truths, and made clear the logic of both: nothing exists, everything exists. He who succeeds in understanding the profound truth of this paradox will achieve the balance that can be worth all or nothing, zero or infinity: Nirvana. Everything exists and nothing exists: everything that is made up of atoms and cells, everything that is thought, that is believed in. Thought is a powerful force, and matter too, since it also is an arrangement of electric forces, or, as the Buddha called them, delicate heat impulses. Therefore everything exists both as a fact in itself and as a projection of our thought, as a sum of our suppositions or beliefs. Yet our senses, and our judgements, are fallible, and they can lead us to consider as real this world of appearances that is, in fact, the sum of the errors that we constantly commit. Do we believe that matter is solid and immutable? On the contrary, it is flowing with energy, a composition of atoms and vacuum (according to the Buddha); our own body, through whose senses we judge other bodies, is in a continuous state of change, has reality in the passing instant, but not in the past or the future, nor is it the same from moment to moment. So we must put our trust in thought: only concentration and meditation lead to the development of one's faculties. By acting according to one's thoughts, by living a succession of right actions, one attains perfection of one's inner self, but not yet a complete solution. Right actions, for example, can create a "system of morals" which is as harmful as vice when it becomes a set of rules. The Buddha taught, therefore, that it is necessary to conquer oneself continually as each stage of spiritual perfection is reached. This is the unique road that leads to Truth; and Truth is salvation. "Unique" because a code of laws for all life does not exist: having ascertained his point of departure, each man must seek out the route for himself, for the experience of others will be of no use to him.

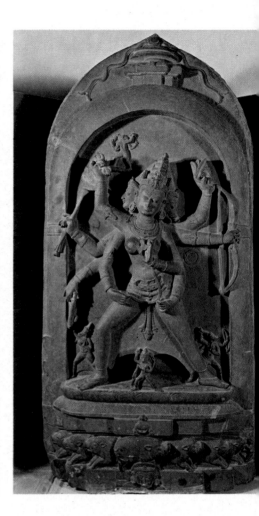

LIFE TOO IS A CONTINUOUS FLOW OF ENERGY

First of all, the Buddha demonstrated that the body is a collection of changing cells and defective senses: an earthly habitation that cannot lead to the Truth. He then showed that it was also impossible for the spirit to participate in this Truth without giving up its conquests and, in the final analysis, itself; for the spirit too is a collection of passing and changing sensations that constitute a fictitious, non-existent "I", in other words, a grand illusion. If the body and spirit cannot serve man, what then is the principle by which man exists? For the Buddha, it is an energy that passes in a continuous flow from one animate object to another: when one being dies another instantly assumes that being's energy. According to his teaching, one should be able to succeed in blocking the flow of individual energy; that is to say, to exhaust the battery without recharging another, while the exhausted battery (the body) is dissolved in other matter. It then reaches Nirvana ("nir va": to be blown out). When questioned about the entity of Nirvana, he made no reply: it

must, in fact, be reached after having passed along the doctrinal path, the "path of explanations". But to provide an adequate definition of Nirvana, one must already have reached it. However, modern science recognizes what the Buddha defined as the "state of non-being". He spoke thus: "There exists a not-born, not-become, not-made, not-compounded; and if this did not exist, it would not be possible to save oneself from what is born, become, made, compounded." By the same principle of opposites, what exists in this world corresponds to what does not exist in an anti-world. The Buddha succeeded, therefore, 2,500 years ago, in asserting the existence of anti-matter, a concept which holds out great promise for the future. Other theories, founded in religious experience but scientific in substance, followed this first one. "As a chariot does not exist in itself, but is made up of various components, so nothing exists in itself, but everything is interrelated; the whole Universe is in correlation." This relativity is all-embracing. Thus the soul is subject to continuous changes of mood; our understanding is subject to the inaccurate perception of our senses; salvation depends on the path that we can each trace for ourselves. "As a monkey fleeing through the forest grasps a branch and then lets it go, then takes hold of another and then another, so, my disciples, what you call your spirit, thought, or understanding, is continually formed and then dissolved." He also said: "He who has understood, judges sand and gold to be of equal value. The sky and the palm of his hand are identical in his eyes."

40

A few of the gods of the Buddhist Pantheon who were not mentioned by the Enlightened One, but were later conceived as concrete Materializations of his philosophical, scientific and transcendental ideas, are represented here. They are, from left to right: Khadivarani Tara, or Mercy, which is a product of compassion (Varendra Museum, Rajshahi); Avalokitesvara, or Personified Compassion (15th-century Nepalese bronze); Marici, goddess of the dawn, riding on the chariot of the eclipse, with symbols of astronomical events (Archaeological Museum, Mainamati); Drakupolo, guardian of the sciences (Potala, Lhasa); Mara, the great illusion (13th century, in wood). In his various states of holiness and enlightenment, the Buddha was given different forms and attributes; they reflect specific meanings with extremely subtle distinctions.

Above: The place where the
Buddha's first five companions, and
possibly the Buddha himself,
preached at Sarnath. The simple
construction of clay bricks built
in their honour by King Asoka was
brought to light during archaeological excavations by the Maha
Bodhi Society in 1931.

Right: A satirical Japanese
print showing the beneficial
effects of a Buddhist sermon on the
hearers: sinners are hastening to
give back their ill-gotten gains,
to take off their shirts and offer
them to the monk, to wipe out
long-standing bad debts or rub out
licentious verse. Other
penitents are weeping, begging
forgiveness, and scattering
alms (Ukiyo-Ye School,
19th century).

BRILLIANT LIGHTNING

Left: Sermon given by the Buddha, who raises his left hand in the gesture of protection, while several women bring offerings and gifts (Archaeological Museum, Taxila). Right: The Buddha preaching as he walks, in a manner reminiscent of Socrates (Central Museum, Lahore). The Greek philosopher was born shortly after the Buddha's death.

For the Buddha, therefore, there is no truth to be found in the sterile examination of first causes, nor any exact science in the observation of the senses. We say "my" book, "my" clothes, "I" have broken a nail, thus creating a fictitious "I" which we maintain although it is in substance nothing. There remains the concept of "relativity", in which Gautama not only preceded Einstein but actually went far beyond him, since, for the Enlightened One, it is even relative to itself. But the Buddha also said: "I declare to you that within the body, although it is mortal and only six feet long, you can find the world, and the origin of the world, and the end of the world, and the path that leads to all goals." And yet again he explained the physical essence of the world, in a series of sermons delivered without interruption for ninety days. Gradually, as the years passed, the Buddha's words were either memorized or written down. The Pali language of the "Abhidharma", the oldest canon, certainly dates from the last years of the Enlightened One's life. According to the Buddha, the Cosmos is energy or manifestation of energy in continuous movement: positive and negative charges set off successive phenomena, and the end of one is linked to the beginning of another. The Cosmos consists of an infinite number of miniature universes, from the atom to the solar systems; it is subject to the law of contraction, which creates mass; and to the law of repetition, through which the universe is in a state of continual expansion. The principal element of its formation is energy, which is in the form of electro-magnetic radiation and is completely interchangeable with mass. Planets, some even bigger than the Earth and inhabited by peoples in a higher stage of evolution, and stars, and satellites, are all born, live and die one after another, their lives lasting millions and millions of years. The atom contains a balance of positive and negative charges. If, by some process, the atom can be split, each unit releases energy, by the immediate and dramatic repetition of nuclear fission in a chain reaction, in what the Buddha called "devavajra" (brilliant lightning): our atomic bomb. Its rotatory movement is 176,470,000,000 revolutions per flash.

43

ANCIENT WISDOM, MODERN SCIENCE

Units of energy are given off by the elements in interplanetary migration: this is what we call radiation. The differences in matter depend on the number of units that make up the atom. Besides the unit of matter—the atom—there exist the units of the spirit —or energy—that spin at a constant speed. They unite the atoms, form the cells and give life to them, and from the composition of the cells man is created; they reign over matter, but without matter they do not exist. The rotational speed of the units of energy and of the units of the atom is constant throughout the Universe, while material time varies from zone to zone. This theory of intergalactic differences of time is one of the most recent conceptions in physics in the West. The rotational speed of the Earth also changes every five thousand solar years. To sum up, Gautama gave the following equal times for the whole Universe: three instants of consciousness correspond to one energy-rotation; seventeen energy-rotations correspond to one matter-rotation, or to the rotation of a neutron round a proton. He also declared that there are eight thousand microbes in a glass of water, and that one should sleep with one's head pointing North and one's feet facing South, this being the direction of the magnetic flow of the earth which was, in fact, proved by Faraday in the last century. In the field of psycho-analysis, the Buddha's notions were in keeping with the introspective speculations of his time. He conceived that images were configurations created by the senses and recorded by the memory, but that they could not be located in any one part of the body, as all parts of it are sensitive. Finally, he said that man is a body containing fifty-two forces; these he duly catalogued.

Opposite page: The monk Zenmui, forerunner of the Tendai sect in Japan; 12th-century Japanese painting (Ichijo-Yi, Hyogo). Above, from left to right: A crowd of Japanese pilgrims worshipping; a Chinese "arhant" (who, according to legend, knew how to bring the dead back to life) accomplishes a chemical miracle (a Japanese painting in the Zen manner, attributed to Mu Ch'in); the monk and chemist, Genzi, master of Kukai, founder of the esoteric Shingon sect, in a 12th-century Japanese painting (Fumon-in, Wakayama). Above: The physicist Taissu contemplating Mount Fuji.

The Buddha thus preached a rational explanation of the whole Universe to his followers, ranging from the smallest molecule to the infinity of the Cosmos, from the cell to the most perfect aggregate of cells: man. He gave an explanation of causes and effects, of the reason for existence, which was highly comprehensive and logical and refuted all argument, yet which at the same time was open to many different interpretations. The Buddha, however, went beyond matters pertaining to religion, philosophy and even science, and advised man to use all means for gaining the goal and then to abandon them as soon as it was achieved, "as a man leaves a raft when he reaches the other bank". He led not only a contemplative but also a practical life, persuading men to follow him beyond any ties of faith. He revealed the practical side of his will in his relationships with both the lay people and the monks: on the former he imposed fixed ethical ways of thought and a well-defined moral code of behaviour; whereas the latter he organized into a community by grouping them into various monasteries (vihara), but without appointing leaders. This seems strange: as a member of the noble warrior caste, he knew about military organization and the advantages of hierarchy; but he insisted that all monks should be equal, and that none consider himself superior in wisdom, knowledge, sanctity or rank to any of the others. The only distinction lay between masters and disciples, that is to say, between those whose task it was to teach and those set to learn. "He who has knowledge does not retain a part of his knowledge in his closed fist; in the same way, he who has knowledge knows that he cannot be at the head of the Order."

Above: The Buddha, accompanied by Vajrapani, converses with an ascetic; the Buddha receives a sheaf of grass from the Hindu god Indra (Peshawar Museum). Above, right: Detail of an Indian miniature using symbols to depict the Hindu gods Rama and Krishna, according to early Buddhist conceptions. Opposite page: Theory of the creation of the universe according to a Tibetan mandala. The cardinal points and the basic forms of the Universe are represented by the appropriate divinities. The Buddha gave a clear definition of the Cosmos to his disciples, explaining atoms, heavenly bodies and their mutual attractions to each other. Each of these parts was then given the name of a divinity.

THE BUDDHIST MONK

Opposite page: The Temple of Dawn at Bangkok.
Below: A monk's refectory, and a school of the Order in Thailand. Monastic discipline (Vinaya) is described in great detail, from admission up to the highest duties, in the Twenty Treatises of the Vinaya which make up the first three books of the Tripitaka. The table is open to the ordinary public who can share the monks' vegetarian meal. They usually eat only one meal a day, before noon, and they are forbidden to take any food, except liquid, in the afternoon. Every morning the monks beg for alms, which are the only source of their provisions and on which they are entirely dependent.

The Buddha set up monasteries that even today are very much like universities. He considered thought to be energy, and he was convinced that he could increase its power and store it in the same way as we now store electric energy, first of all in a single individual by means of suitable exercises and concentration, then by a union of these individuals, thus creating a "working force". Therefore it is useful for humanity that a certain number of persons embrace a way of life leading to spiritual enlightenment. The novice (samanera) enters the Order at not less than 16 years of age, has his head shaved and learns the Ten Buddhist Precepts: do not take life, do not take what is not given you, do not commit adultery, tell no lies and deceive no one, do not drink alcohol, eat temperately and not at all in the afternoon, do not watch dancing, nor listen to singing or plays, wear no garlands, perfumes or any adornments, do not sleep in luxurious beds, accept no gold or silver. At 20, if he is celibate, healthy and without debts, he becomes an ordained monk (bhikkhu). He then touches with a staff the gifts offered to him: three cotton robes (yellow or orange, according to the place), a razor, a needle, a water filter, and a begging bowl; he will own nothing else. He is bound by no vows, and if he desires he can return to ordinary society. Fornication, theft, murder and fraud are grounds for immediate dismissal from the Order. The monk attends two monthly meetings, on the day of the new moon and on the day of the full moon. At these he listens to the 227 rules that he must observe and he publicly confesses his sins. But if a monk fails to carry out his proper duties, the ordinary people from whom he begs his food will reject and scorn him. In general, Buddhist religious practice has little in common with Western practice. At its heart lie the worship of sacred relics and statues, the pilgrimage to recognized shrines such as Kapilavastu, Bodh Gaya, Sarnath (Benares) and Kusinara, and the sermon. Monasteries vary in construction: in the North they are enclosed by stone walls, whereas in the South unenclosed pagodas are found. In contrast to Hindu temples, which are strictly forbidden to non-believers, Buddhist monasteries are open to all, whatever their faith.

Below: The death of the Buddha represented in a Japanese painting (1086, Kongobu-ji, Wakayama); and in a Gandharan sculpture. Opposite page: Detail of the Japanese painting, with kings and demons weeping at the death of the Buddha. Many legends turned the last moments of the Enlightened One into a series of miraculous happenings: the gods of heaven and earth came to weep at the death of their spiritual lord; the earth trembled and the sky grew dark, while even the animals were grief-stricken and worshipped the revered corpse. At a more realistic level, the Buddha's death may be compared with the death of Socrates about a century later.

DEATH OF THE BUDDHA

It was the rainy season when Gautama felt the first strong pains. He sent messengers to all the vihara convoking the monks to Kusinara in three months' time. Then he turned to Ananda and said: "Today I have reached the great age of eighty, and my body is like a rickety old chariot. Did I not tell you right at the beginning of my preaching that nothing on earth resists ruin and death? In the highest of the ethereal heavens, in the Heaven whose essence is beyond conception, a life of many millions of centuries is lived, but even there everything has an end, everything perishes. Because of this, I have revealed the knowledge that destroys the roots of life and death. Nor, after my Nirvana, will this knowledge perish with me." When the moment came, he set off for the last meeting-place. In the Mango Wood near Pava, at the house of the blacksmith Cunda, he ate contaminated food which enfeebled him further. He continued on his way and met the nobleman Putkasa, an old pupil of Alara, and converted him, receiving from him as a gift two rolls of cloth of gold. He put them on, and then bathed in the waters of the Katutstha. At last he arrived at Sala Wood near Kusinara. He spoke at great length to the faithful, clarifying his doctrine and his conception of the Order, exhorting them to do good and constantly seek the Truth. "After my death," he said, "preach what is right, do good, behave rightly. Wherever things are done well, I shall be found." Then the families of the Malla were presented to him, and he blessed them, and then he blessed the monks. Turning to them, he continued: "I am entering Nirvana; if you have any doubts about the Doctrine, question me now, so that controversy and argument may not divide you later." But the monks answered that they had no doubts. The Buddha then addressed an old man of 120 and recapitulated the Four Truths, adding: "All created things perish and die, even the Tathagata. Work without ceasing for your salvation." He had Ananda prepare a couch for him, and he lay down on it, and turned his head towards the North. His spirit, so the texts say, passed through the four highest levels of knowledge. Whereupon the Buddha died; and the earth trembled, and the light of day grew dim, and princes and monks wept, and trees shed their foliage.

Below: Detail of a Japanese painting representing the Buddha's deaths. Bottom: Ananda's statue watching over the Buddha's passing, 12th-century rock sculpture at Palonnaruwa (Ceylon). Ananda assisted the Enlightened One from the time of his own conversion until the end, and the Buddha's last words were addressed to him.

The Dharmarajika stupa, erected by the Emperor Asoka at Sarnath to contain the Buddha's relics. It is probably an enlargement of the original stupa. Archaeological research has revealed other stupas, all considerably altered and embellished at various periods, and for this reason it is difficult to say if the relics these monuments contain are those of the Buddha or of other saints. More than 3,000 stupas were built after the Buddha's death in countries where the Buddhist faith penetrated. Naturally they do not all contain relics of the Buddha or of saints, but some preserve sacred texts and statues. Bottom: Worshipping relics in Bangkok.

Left: Various representations of the Buddha. A Chinese statue in gilded stucco (Yuan epoch, 1280–1367); a wooden statue depicting Avalokitesvara, Northern China, 12th century; a Buddha in solid gold weighing eight tons, worshipped at Bangkok. Thai, 13th century; a Buddha in gilded wood, Southern China, 18th century; Avalokitesvara in painted wood, Western China, Ming era; Buddha in glazed ceramic, Imperial China, Ming dynasty, (1368–1643); Buddha with disciples in a Tibetan temple. Far bottom left: worshipping relics at Bangkok.
Below: A large Chinese statue in porcelain, Ming era, end of 15th century.

DISPUTE OVER THE MORTAL REMAINS OF THE BUDDHA

Seven days after the death of the Buddha, the Malla princes of Kusinara bore the body to the southern ramparts of the city, where it was cremated with all the honours due to a great sovereign. The story goes that the pyre ignited and extinguished itself, while a strong scent of jasmine pervaded the air. The Malla then carried the remains to a sanctuary within their palace. But kings, princes, and the faithful from other districts came flocking to the palace, and pressed their more or less valid claims to the remains. Among them were the superstitious Sakya, King Ajatasatru, the Licchavi of Vaisali, the Bulaka of Calikalpa, the Kaudya of Ramagrama, the Malla of Pava, and the Brahmins of Visnudvija. Many seized arms, and invested the city when the lords of Kusinara refused to hand over the revered remains. Those without painted their elephants with warpaint, those within set close ranks of archers to defend the walls of the capital. At that point, a Brahmin, Dhumrasa Gotra, recalled the words of peace spoken so many times by the Buddha and his desire for non-violence. He proposed to settle the dispute thus: "Let the seven kings build seven stupas measuring four cubits to contain seven parts of the remains; and let us trust an eighth part to the Naga serpents in the heart of the forest. And let us raise one stupa for the begging bowl and one for the ashes of the pyre." This was agreed, and peace was restored. The relics were placed inside caskets of gold and rock-crystal. These were enclosed in silver boxes, which in their turn were placed in bronze containers, and the whole was set in an urn made of stone or pottery, over which a stupa was erected. A stupa is a tomb in the shape of a high tumulus which gradually becomes more and more richly adorned with sculptured decorations and symbolic superstructures. Not all the ten original stupas have yet been located, probably because many of the early structures have been overlaid by later embellishments. The relics contained in a crystal phial in the stupa at Bhattibrolu were given to the Maha Bodhi Society by Lord Ronaldhay, Viceroy of India, when the structure was restored, and they are revered today in a vihara built specially at Calcutta. Other relics are at Gandhara and, perhaps, at Sarnath and Sanchi.

"PROCLAIM THE GLORIOUS DOCTRINE."

"Proclaim the glorious Doctrine, preach a way of pure and perfect sanctity", said the Buddha to his disciples. Buddhism was to become the first religion to assume a universal character. The effective beginning of the story was the conversion of the great king Asoka Maurya (*c.* 274–236 B.C.), who came to be known as the "Constantine of Buddhism". Asoka united India into a single great empire, but only after a series of cruel battles. One evening, as he stood on Dhauli hill contemplating his conquered enemies sprawled in a river of blood, he was smitten with remorse and determined to embrace the religion of non-violence. So he imposed the Dharma upon his new empire and himself ruled over it with enlightened benevolence. He spread Buddhism throughout India, and sent missionaries as far as Asia Minor and, it is said, to Gaul, Greece and England. In 253 B.C., his son (or brother) Mahinda brought the faith to Ceylon, which remains to this day the home of fundamental Buddhism. In India the great King Kaniska of the Indo-Afghan dynasty of the Kushana Scyths and King Harsa continued to propagate the faith. But after the death of the latter, there began a slow decline. Buddhism spread into China from the 1st century A.D. onwards, and it continued to expand until about the 6th century. In 220 A.D. it gained a hold in Vietnam, and a little more than a hundred years later, in Korea, from where it spread to Japan. There it became the state religion. At the same time it permeated into Burma, where it is still the official religion today. In 650, the first temple was erected in Tibet; from there Buddhism passed into Mongolia. There followed a slow decline throughout Asia, either because of fierce and systematic persecution, as in China, or because of the advance of Hinduism, whose character tended to satisfy the ignorant masses. Buddhism made its first impact on Western civilization in the wake of the British conquest of India. At the end of the 18th century, Elena Blavatsky introduced Buddhist theory to the Theosophical Society. The Buddhist Society of Great Britain was set up in London in 1906. Meanwhile, Asian immigrants to the New World created important centres of the Dharma. Throughout the world today there are some 168,389,000 Buddhists.

Left: Pilaster of King Asoka, on the exact spot where he prayed at Sarnath, after he had become a monk towards the end of his life. It is in the centre of the large group of monastic buildings which the pious king had built, and which have been brought to light during recent archaeological excavations.
Left, below: Indo-Greek coin depicting King Eucratides (about 175 B.C.), and coin of the Scytho-Afghan King Vasuveda Kushana (217–244), monarchs who contributed to the later expansion of Buddhism. Left, bottom: Tumulus erected at Pataliputra (the modern Patna, in the Bihar) over the body of Asoka's brother whom the King himself killed before his conversion to Buddhism.
This page: An enormous stone elephant which King Asoka had sculptured on Dhauli hill (Orissa), at the spot where he was converted to Buddhism. On the elephant's flank a long inscription, said to have been written by the King, records the event.

COUNCILS AND DISSIDENTS

Opposite: Buddhist monks from the South at Bangkok. The dialectics of the later Councils did not appeal to the monks of the South; they adhere to this day to a doctrine formulated at the First and Second Councils, and more akin to the original Dharma than that of the sects of the North.

As the Dharma spread, the character of Buddhism itself underwent change. From being a philosophy of life here on earth and beyond with the gods, it gradually became a religion to which had been attached a chaotic assortment of divinities. Almost immediately after the Buddha's death, about 500 monks met near Rajaghra to codify the rules of the Enlightened One. According to information handed down to us, Kasyapa, the chief exponent at the meeting, drafted the doctrine, Ananda the sermons (Sutra), and Upali the rules of monastic discipline (Vinaya). This First Council (*c.* 473 B.C.) was followed by another, 130 years later. At the Second Council, at Vaisali, some seven hundred monks rebelled against the early heretics of the Great Community, on the ground that the restrictions imposed by the elders (sthavira) were intolerable. These monks formed the first important dissident group (Mahasanghika). In the 3rd century B.C., the Emperor Asoka organized the Third Council at Pataliputra (Patna). Only the elders took part in this, and it was they who classified the canonical texts collected in the so-called Three Baskets of Wisdom (Tipitaka). King Kaniska (about 78–103 A.D.) convoked a Fourth Council at Jalandhara in the Punjab and at Kundalavana in Kashmir, to interpret the basic tenets of the Mahasanghika, which had become the most widespread and accepted form of Buddhism. Since 1950, when the World Fellowship of Buddhists was formed at Colombo, international congresses have been held every second year. They are open to all sects because "right is the marrow of all the sects".

Above, left: A covered building on the archaeological site at Pataliputra, at the spot where Asoka is said to have summoned the Third Council.
Centre: Two Japanese "mandapa" (portable shrines) represent the Guardian of the East (above) and the Guardian of the West. Conceived by the Buddha, divinities of this order had come to be widely accepted by the time of

the Fourth Council (1st century A.D.).
Above, right: Bronze bell in a Tibetan temple, and a satirical Japanese print depicting a thief coveting a temple gong. Temple adornments were introduced after the Third Council in the middle of the 3rd century B.C. This was the Council convened by Asoka, the "Constantine of Buddhism", and presided over by the venerable Tissa.

Below: A flying angel (Apsara); fresco in a grotto at Tun-Huang in Central Asia. Centre: Buddhist divinity in mandarin costume, 10th-century Chinese painting from Tun-Huang (British Museum, London); the Buddha surrounded by bodhisattvas, 6th-century sculpture in the grottoes of Lung Men-in-China; emanation from an archetypal Buddha (Adibuddha), painting from Central Asia (Guimet Museum, Paris); and sculpture representing a monk worshipping the three bodies of the Buddha, from Tun-Huang (Guimet Museum, Paris). Right: Lubliubi teaching the Dharma to Naga and Garuda, 19th-century Tibetan painting (Guimet Museum, Paris).

HINAYANA: THE SMALLER VEHICLE

As Buddhism spread into areas beyond the Ganges valley, the word of the Buddha reached different races of people, who practised other customs and habits, and lived in diverse conditions and environments. The peoples of the South, for instance, who were more attracted to contemplation than to speculative ideas, were not affected by dialectics, but held to the genuine original Dharma. Other peoples, who were perhaps less advanced or were under the influence of mythology and superstition, added their own demons and legends to Buddhism. Further substantial deviations from the original doctrine occurred when it came into contact with the lower social orders who were perhaps more primitive and simple-minded. Thus countless different interpretations led to the formation of sects and faiths which, in the end, came into open conflict with each other. Geographic dispersion meant that the Dharma was affected by that impermanence within whose clutches the Buddha placed all worldly things; but it also obliged many centres, which were left to go their own way after conversion, to evolve in an autonomous manner. In general, Buddhism split into three main streams: Theravada, Mahayana and Vajrayana. The first, which still flourishes in the Southern countries (Ceylon, Burma, Siam, Laos and Cambodia), upheld the orthodox image of the earliest form of Buddhism. It is the so-called "Ancient School of Wisdom" organized in an analytical manner by Sariputra, one of the Enlightened One's best pupils. Theravada, which is disparagingly called by the other schools the Smaller Vehicle (Hinayana), is based on the classical triad: Buddha the master, Dharma the doctrine, and Sangha the order of monks. It is, one might say, historical and anti-nominalistic. For example, it lays little stress on divinities or spirits; it also believes in the instability of phenomena, in universal suffering caused by life, and in rebirth from which one can free oneself by reaching Nirvana. It follows the "Noble Eightfold Path", practises Right Behaviour as advocated by the Buddha, obeys his Five Precepts, and aspires to his Ten Perfections. In China, the Lu Tsung sect and the Ch'eng-Shih Tsung sect belonged to the Hinayana; in Japan, the Kusha, the Jojitsu and the Ritsu.

Below: Two 19th-century Japanese engravings by Hiroshige: a "toril" (from the Indian "torana": portal); and the open space in a Buddhist temple. Bottom: Illustrations from a 17th-century Zen text. The buffalo symbolizes Truth, while the herdsman who looks for or leads him symbolizes the Soul. Zen is the most surrealistic and

unpredictable Buddhist sect; for it aims to disconcert the mind in order to liberate it from earthly impurities.
Opposite: Devotions of a Buddhist monk in China (1901); the Gallery of Buddhas in the Monastery at Bangkok.

MAHAYANA: THE GREAT VEHICLE

The doctrine of the Ancient School was considered by some Buddhists to be incomplete in form and unsatisfying in practice, and a new discipline developed to examine the Hinayana canons in depth and to broaden their concepts. Did this perhaps confirm the Enlightened One's prophecy? Although he was opposed to the admission of women into the Order, he foresaw that their acceptance would become a fact and the Dharma would only remain intact for five hundred years. But as its influence spread, a greater popularization of the Dharma became essential; and as its popularity grew, so it was inevitable that it should acquire a religious and esoteric character, and cast off its true intellectual and atheistic nature. The ideal man is now no longer the saint (arhant) who becomes holy for his own sake alone, but he who, reaching the threshold of Nirvana, does not pass over, but turns back to save those who remain in Illusion. Such is the bodhisattva. This ideal of the sacrifice of self was extended even to the Buddha, and a multitude of reincarnate forms were found for him. One of these, Avalokitesvara (in Chinese, Kuan Yin; in Japanese, Kannon), is now the most widely worshipped divinity of all. The Mahayana, or "Great Vehicle", also brought new life to Buddhism on the doctrinal level through its great thinkers, among whom were Nagarjuna (1st-2nd century), inventor of the theory of the vacuity of things and father of relativism; Asanga (5th century), expounder of monistic scripture and idealizer of the absolute; Santideva (7th century), poet of mysticism. The Mahayana penetrated mainly into China, Korea and Japan. In these countries, development was based on the freedom permitted by the theory of "continuous becoming", and Buddhism split into many schools which greatly enriched it. The "School of the Pure Land" worshipped Amitabha, through whom believers might enter paradise. In contrast, the Zen School was based on strenuous mystical discipline. Other schools were the Sino-Japanese Hosso schools, founded by Dosho; Sanron; Kegon (which is practised in the Todai-ji, the largest wooden building in the world, where a statue of the Buddha 36 feet high is worshipped); the all-embracing Tendai; the esoteric Shingon; and the purist Nichiren.

An epigram expresses the surrealistic teachings of Zen. A master said to his pupil: "Do not call this a jar. How would you call it?" The pupil, in reply, overturned the jar and left the room. "Two Hands clapped together make a sound. What sound does one hand make?" "If there is no god, where is god?" Reply: "All is god." "If I come to you empty-handed, what do you say to me?" asked the pupil. "Throw it away," replied the master. "But if I have nothing?" "Well bring it to me if you want to." A master asked his pupils: "If I say that a goose is in a bottle, what do you do to free it?" And after several wrong answers: "Say it is free."

Below: Tibetan lamas praying in the Potala at Lhasa to chase away demons; they wave small bells shaped like a fork of lightning and read "mantra" (formulae).
Right: A monk in the Potala at Lhasa blowing a long trumpet to chase away demons. Behind him is a row of prayer wheels.

Right: A prayer wheel and a small trumpet. Both have a ritual purpose. The trumpet, which is from the Potala, was used to drive away demons bringing bad luck. The wheel contains twelve pages with forty-one lines of text, each with the prayer-formula "Om mani padme Hum" written sixty times, making a total of 29,520 times. By rotating the prayer wheel 120 times a minute, 3,542,400 prayers rise to heaven in that time. In Tibet big wooden prayer wheels are connected to water-falls and water-courses; perpetually moving, they send endless prayers up to heaven. Far right: a monk disguised as a demon dancing to drive out evil spirits.

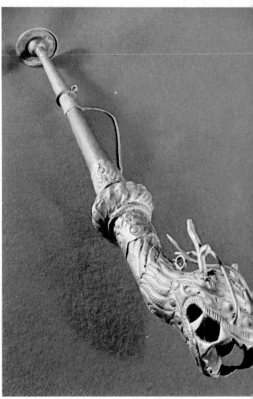

MAGIC AND THE RITUAL "VEHICLE"

About the 6th century, the rules of procedure and magical process prevalent at that time in Mahayanistic India were made into collections (tantra). Under the growing influence of yoga, specific practices such as the control of respiratory rhythm were defined, while surviving pagan influences attached importance to magic syllables (mantra), for by pronouncing them in a certain manner one could enter into the Absolute. Such esoteric and magical formulae, which were first practised sporadically in Tibet at the time of King Sron btsan sgam po (died 649), now developed autonomously in India and led to the creation of the Tantric Vehicle, or the Diamond Vehicle, also known as Mantrayana (Ritual Vehicle). Legions of devils were added to divinities and bodhisattvas, all of which were incarnations of fragments of the Universal Soul; sometimes they were good or harmless, more often hostile and terrible. The two Buddhist wives of Sron btsan sgam po, the first, Nepalese, the second, Chinese, by whom the Court was converted, were deified as Green Tara and White Tara, protectresses of Tibet. By the reign of King K'ri sron lde btsan (742–797), the Vehicle had already made a great impression on the people through the agency of the monk Padma Sambhava; by about 1040, it had taken complete control. The people believed that many miraculous feats might be achieved: control of the elements, levitation, telepathy, teletransport, resistance to intense cold, and so on. On a practical level, the monks gradually assumed temporal power until eventually they were in complete control of the government. The chief personality in this religious supremacy was Tsong Ka-Pa (1358–1419), who was responsible for the reform that set up the two opposing groups: the Yellow Hats (monks of the right hand, who might not marry), and the Red Hats (monks of the left hand, who were permitted to do so). It seems that the institution of the Dalai Lama (dalai: great ocean; la-ma: higher), or king-priest, was also due to him, as well as that of the Panchen Lama, or chief administrator, who governed until the Chinese Invasion. The sexual element in the Red Hats, which developed from the theory of the Pair of Opposites, led to the creation of a series of female divinities, according to a theory called Shaktism.

DIVINITIES WITHOUT NUMBER

Something like a deification of the Buddha was established in the Great Vehicle, a multiplicity of his images were created in the Tantric Vehicle, and now the Buddhist pantheon was further enriched by the personification of Gautama's acts and thoughts. The figuration encompasses the various moments of his life (meditation, enlightenment, human charity, teaching, the Wheel of the Law, etc.), and each is represented in its own specific posture. Then an essential trinity is defined: created body (nirmana-kaya) with which he came down to earth; spiritual body (sambhoga-kaya) with which he entered heaven; and truth-body (dharma-kaya) which is his identity in the Absolute. These bodies later became in their turn individual essences. From them the "original Buddha" (Adibuddha) takes its value and being, the "always existing", from which concept the five dhyanibuddhas (Akshobhya, Amitabha, Amoghasiddhi and Ratnasambhava at the four cardinal points, Vairocana at the centre) are born, from whom in their turn emanate the five dhyanibodhisattvas. One of these is Avalokitesvara, who is highly revered as a god of mercy and a saviour. Among the Buddhas of the future Maitreya is highly revered, while past Buddhas number from 4 to 32, depending on the school. Then there are eight archangels, and below them numerous guardian divinities, furies, custodians and demons; and, lower still the 36 Brahma divinities that have to submit to the laws of metempsychosis. At the Eastern cardinal alone, say the Tibetans, who give to each divinity its female counterpart, there are half a million myriads of Buddhas.

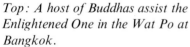

Top: A host of Buddhas assist the Enlightened One in the Wat Po at Bangkok.
Below this, left:
Saptakotibuddha-matra, the "Mother of all Buddhas", Japanese painting on the central pillar of the five-level pagoda of Daigo-ji (Kyoto), 10th century; and right: Gold plaque depicting the "100,000 Buddhas in heaven" (Siam, 15th century).
Centre: Two arhant in a 19th-century Japanese illustration.

Opposite: A representation of the Buddhist hierarchy in two arrangements: the Vajradhatu or spiritual circle, and the Garbhadatu or material circle; detail of a 9th-century Japanese painting. As well as a multiplicity of images there was also one of names, which were pronounced and written differently by every nation. As often as possible, the names in this book have been written in Sanskrit, but they are different in Pali, Tibetan, Chinese and Japanese.

Below: Two pages from a 16th-century Tibetan book written on gold-leaf (in the Potala at Lhasa).
Right: Illustration from the Astasahasrika Prajnaparamita (perfect wisdom) which is 8,000 verses long, 11th–12th-century Pala miniature (Victoria and Albert Museum, London).
Opposite page, top: Chinese library of wooden tablets at Ch'engtu, Wen Shu Yüan. Each tablet has two engraved sides. The oldest date back to about 350 A.D., and prints have been taken from them through the centuries, by pressing down a fine sheet of mulberry-silk paper on to the inked tablets. These texts have therefore had an incalculable number of copies printed from them.
Centre: Buddha in the centre of the Chinese pantheon; frontispiece of a Buddhist book printed in the 10th century or earlier (Bibliothèque Nationale, Paris).
Bottom: A large Buddhist painting from Tun Huang with a long text beneath.

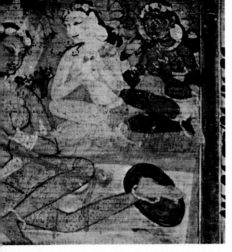

THE LITERATURE OF BUDDHISM

The 2,500 years of Buddhist doctrine has produced a rich literary harvest, with a vast body of commentaries on the canonical texts, and an even vaster amount of historical, hagiographical and doctrinal amplifications. India and Japan possess the longest and the greatest number of poems in the world.

An unlimited number of divine images have been created from the figure of the Buddha, and in the same way a vast literature has been written round his sermons. The Buddha's biography has been reconstructed by many commentators, essayists and popular writers, who have tried to explain his theories and have recounted the history and development of Buddhism. The oldest printed book that has been handed down to us is a 9th-century Chinese version, printed on a tablet, of the Diamond-Cutter Sutra, now preserved in the British Museum. In the same century the Buddhist University of Nalanda (which 8,500 pupils and 1,500 masters used to attend every year and where a hundred lessons were given every day) preserved in its library, which has been called the richest in the world, a copy of each lesson. In 1905 R. J. Jackson and J. R. Pain opened in London the first European bookshop dedicated to Buddhist literature in the English language. The common origin of all texts was the canon in the Pali language which was compiled between the First and Second Councils. It is divided into three parts (Tipitaka: three baskets); the Vinaya Pitaka, which contains the rules of the Order and is divided in its turn into five books; the Sutta Pitaka, or collection of sermons, which likewise is divided into five volumes with more than 4,000 Suttas; and in the Abhidhamma Pitaka, the Basket of Metaphysical Knowledge, that contains in seven treatises all the philosophical and scientific ideas of the Buddha. One of the most important commentators of the Tipitaka was Buddhaghosa, who wrote the Visuddhi Magga (Path of Purification). In addition to the Tipitaka, the Smaller Vehicle studies the post-canonical Milinda Panha, or Questions, that the Indo-Greek King Milinda (Menandros) put to the sage Nagasena. The Great Vehicle added many other texts in Sanskrit to the canon: for example the Mahavastu and the Divyavadana. In Tibet, the Kanjur, with 108 volumes, and the Tanjur, with 250 volumes, as well as the Mahamudra of the first Tashi-Lama and treatises on occult science like the Kui-ti, with 35 volumes of text and 14 of commentary, are all read. Each sect has brought to the already enormous quantity of the original its own weighty contribution.

Left: Head of the Buddha in green jade; Tonkin, 15th century. Below: A Burmese bronze head, 16th century – the curls turn in the direction of the sun's course – and three Japanese heads: Gakko, 8th-century sculpture (Todaiji, Nara); Kannon, 8th-century carved wood (Horyuji, Nara); Miroku, 7th-century wood (Koryuji, Kyoto).

BUDDHIST ART IN INDIA

Ananda once said to the Buddha: "One half of a saintly life is friendship, association and intimacy with the Beautiful". To which the Buddha replied: "Do not say that, Ananda. This constitutes the *whole* of a saintly life. A monk who feels amity, affinity and intimacy with Beauty can be expected to follow the Noble Eightfold Path and to make good use of it." Thus the Buddha's attitude towards art was codified and its importance recognized. It was perhaps due to this that Buddhist art, which was born and developed in India, in the first place influenced many peoples who did not have an aesthetic sense, and only later inspired a formal evolution. There are, in fact, two clearly-defined periods. The first, the Indian Period, specialized in portraiture,

and the countries of Buddhist faith dependent on India tended to assimilate what the sub-continent taught them. In the second period, Mongolia, China, Tibet, Indochina and Japan created their own styles, becoming more and more successful and mature; while in India Buddhist art began to lose its inspiration. In the first centuries after the death of the Buddha, Indian architecture was of perishable wood, and nothing of it has remained. In due course stone took its place, and under King Asoka a definite and conscious style was evolved. Formal development was intensified in the period of the Sunga (187–75 B.C.), who reconstructed many of the monuments of the preceding period; and in the Andhra period, when the excavation of cave-sanctuaries adorned with marvellous friezes was initiated. The finest period followed (1st–5th centuries), during which the Afghan-Greek Gandhara School the Mathura School and the Amaravati School codified the figure of the Buddha in classical statuary and the rock sanctuaries were covered with magnificent frescoes. Finally there followed the golden Gupta and post-Gupta period (5th–10th centuries), during which the forms earlier aspired to were fully developed.

A bronze Buddha's head of the 13th-century Sukhotay epoch. One eye is an emerald, the other is of onyx. It was formerly in the Royal Palace at Bangkok. Below: Kannon (Japanese name for Avalokitesvara); ceramic from Satsuma, 1780. This is a rare example of ceramic statuary from the province of Kyushu.

Buddhist art reached its highest classical expression in the Gupta and post-Gupta period (5th-10th centuries). Thereafter the best work was in Ceylon, and subsequently in Indochina, where exceptionally beautiful art forms were created (Khmer, Champa, Sukhotay). In the Indian subcontinent, meanwhile, a decline set in, in face of the prevailing influence of Hindu art. It was magnificent at times, but cold and anonymous, and lacking in that aesthetic sense that drew Indian Buddhist art close to Greek classicism, in a reciprocal relationship of great importance to them both.

69

BUDDHIST ART IN THE FAR EAST

The proliferation of sects, the exposition of their theories, the enormous number of divinities, the necessity for places of worship have all powerfully influenced the development of Buddhists arts everywhere, but the greatest evidence of this can be found in the countries of East Asia. Philosophy and social mores have conditioned attitudes and the tangible expression of aesthetic taste, in China and Japan especially. But from now on, one can speak of Buddhist art as a whole, united in its representation of the Dharma from which all artistic expression is derived. In China, Buddhist art asserted itself between the 1st and 3rd centuries under the Han dynasty and at the time of the Three Kingdoms, during which period sculpture in particular was developed. In the period of the Six Dynasties (317–589), the Indian stupa was transformed. In Tibet it was elevated considerably and a complex cosmogonical value was attributed to it. In China it acquired the pagoda shape that we are familiar with, being built round a central stem with each level sharply defined by decorative roofs. Under the Suei Dynasty (590–617), grandiose works of art in rock were sculptured, and the figure of the Buddha acquired a characteristic stately nobility. Under the T'ang and the Sung (618–1279), monasteries were built in the form of heavy square towers, sculpture was delicate and sensitive, and crafts such as calligraphy took on new vigour. Under the Yuan (1280–1367) rather barbaric but majestic wooden statues were made. The Ming dynasty was notable for the extreme refinement of its art. But then a decline set in and continued under the Ch'ing (1644–1911). Buddhism also had a considerable influence on Japanese art, and developments there have followed their own path. Let us simply mention some individual masterpieces. Among the most outstanding are: the Horyu-ji at Nara (607 A.D.), the most ancient temple still intact in East Asia; the largest wooden temple, the colossal bronze statues of the Buddha, about 35 feet high, at Nara (749) and at Kamakura (1252). We must mention especially a particular School: the Zen, which partly inspired the "bushido" (chivalrous code of the samurai), and from which has come a synthesis of literature that stimulates and inspires thought.

THE BUDDHA STILL LIVES

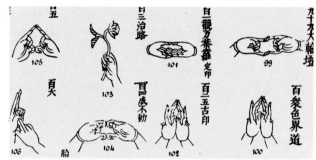

"I have revealed to you," the Buddha said, "as many things as there are leaves on a great tree. But as many things have been revealed to me as there are leaves in a forest." What was the source of his wisdom? Did he reveal the secret knowledge of the Brahmins? Was he the inheritor of the philosophy of some ancient and perfect civilization? Did he comprehend the Universal Truth through the extreme sensitivity of his own spirit? Or did he perhaps come from another planet, as was said of his contemporary, Mahavira, founder of Jainism? "I have travelled in the heavens that surround the Earth, and I have visited other worlds." But was this an exalted figure of speech or the statement of a fact? These are questions destined to remain for ever unanswered; for the original philosophy is buried beneath a mass of diverse contemporary ritual, and many texts lie unknown to us in Tibetan monasteries. According to the Buddha, each one of us may seek the Truth within himself. And Science may yet disclose the truths hidden in the words of the Enlightened One, "as a lamp that is carried into a dark room allows us to see what is already in there". "I will return to the Earth in 5,000 years time," said the Buddha, "and in the heavens there is the future Buddha, to whom I have already preached the Dharma." Shall we then have to wait for the coming of another cosmic era? If we have understood what the Buddha taught, then we know the true essence of man is his mind and his spirit. Two thousand five hundred years have passed since the Buddha lived – years of misunderstanding and years of persecution – but they have not erased the words of the Buddha, and through them he is with us to this day.

Above left: The Buddha of the future, in monk's robes, worshipping with joined hands the Buddha already come, the Tathagata, who is teaching him the Dharma; 15th-century Chinese statue in gilded wood.
Below left: Suicide of a Buddhist monk in the centre of Saigon (Vietnam, August 1963).

He has soaked himself in petrol, and is letting himself be devoured by the flames in passive protest against President Diem's persecution of the Buddhists.
Centre: An engraving depicting ritual gestures of the Tendai sect.
Below: The statue of Sarnath (Benares), of Anagarika Dharmapala who in 1891

founded the Maha Bodhi Society, a Buddhist organization that helps pilgrims in India and restores the Buddhist sacred places. It has also built schools, temples and libraries. In India, the Buddha's homeland and cradle of the Buddhist faith, his followers now represent only 0.5 per cent of the population.

Sunset over the temples of Bangkok "As the sun goes down, so it returns. Every sunset seems to us its death, but it is a false death. We shall not see its real end, yet one day even the sun will be extinguished," affirmed the Buddha. And when he was at the point of death, he said: "In the Jambudvipa there is a wonderful tree, an udumbara. It bears fruits without flowering, but when it produces golden flowers it will be a sign that a new Buddha will be born into the world." The faithful have deified the Buddha to come, calling him Maitreya. The historical Buddha was called Siddhartha, of the Gautama family, of the Sakya clan. When he became an ascetic he was called Sakyamuni (the wise man of the Sakya); or else Bhagava (he who possesses happiness), or Jina (victorious one), or Tathagata (the thus come, or: he who has attained perfection). When he reached a state of enlightenment (bodhi), he became the Buddha. Among the many other names attributed to him, is the name Amida (the pious one).

Who then was the Buddha? What was his message? He left behind him a way of thought based on a scientific knowledge whose sources we do not know, and he became the head of a religion that he did not found. If he had not existed, he would be the expression of the mightiest aspirations. But he did live, and history proves it, even though the Buddha himself taught how false historic proofs may be and how relative the statements made by men. Before thinkers took possession of his teaching and made it obscure with their elucidations; before human desire for immanence made him into a god; before the desire for the mystical concealed his acts from us under a cloak or miracles and symbols, we could contemplate the man. But he foresaw this situation, and said: "The teachings that you yourselves consider lead to tranquillity and not to passion, to unconcern and not to egotism, to frugality and not to greed, to satisfaction and not to dissatisfaction, to solitude and not to multitude, to energy and not to inertia, to joy in goodness and not in evil – these teachings will tell you with certainty: this is the way, this the discipline, this the message of the Buddha." For the masses, his words provided a moral incentive; and for higher intellects, an invitation to enter into ethical and scientific knowledge.

556 B.C. approx. – Siddhartha Gautama, the future Buddha, is born at Kapilavastu, on the borders of Nepal and India.
540 B.C. approx. – Siddhartha marries his cousin Yasodhara.
529 B.C. – the four encounters. Rahula, son of Siddhartha and Yasodhara, is born. Siddhartha leaves his father's palace and dons the robes of a beggar monk.
519 B.C. – enlightenment at Uruvilva (Bodh Gaya); the first sermon at Sarnath.
479 B.C. – death of Confucius.
476 B.C. – death of the Buddha at Kusinara (Kusia).
473 B.C. approx. – First Council, at Rajaghra.
470–399 B.C. – Socrates.
356–23 B.C. – Alexander the Great.
336 .B.C. – Second Council, at Vaisali.
327 B.C. – Alexander the Great makes an expedition into India.
322 B.C. – death of Aristotle.
321–187 B.C. – Mauryan dynasty governs India.
274–36 B.C. – Reign of King Asoka, first protector of Buddhism. Third Council, at Pataliputra (Patna).
253 B.C. – Mahinda introduces Buddhism to Ceylon.
187 B.C. – the Sunga dynasty succeeds the Mauryan dynasty in India.
25–60 A.D. – Buddhism begins to spread into China.
65 – first document of the Buddhist community in China.
70 – Titus destroys the temple in Jerusalem.
78–103 approx. – Kaniska introduces Buddhism into Central Asia. Fourth Council.
220 – establishment of Buddhism in Vietnam.
249 – the Sassanidae in Gandhara. Gandhara art.
300–400 – first cultural influences penetrate into Japan from Korea

and China (script amongst other things).
317–589 – period of the Six Dynasties in China; the Indian stupa becomes a pagoda built round a central stem.
372–90 – Buddhism dominates in China and Korea.
399–414 – Fa Hsien makes a pilgrimage to India.
420–52 – Buddhist expansion into Burma, Java and Sumatra. First persecution in China.
455–500 – the White Huns invade Gandhara.
552 – Buddhism brought to Japan from Korea.
570–632 – Mohammed.
590–617 – Suei dynasty in China: grandiose sculptures are carved out of rock.
607 – the Horyu-ji temple built at Nara (Japan).
610 – Buddhism becomes the state religion in Japan.
618–1279 – in China, under the T'ang and the Sung, sculpture is delicate and artistic, painting highly spiritual.
629 – Hiuan-tsang's journey to India.
630 – the Koran.
650 – first Buddhist temple in Tibet.
670–749 – Gyogi attempts a syncretism between Buddhism and Shintoism in Japan.
720 – Buddhism spreads into Siam.
750–800 – Buddhist art at Borobudur (Java).
751 – the Arabs conquer the T'ang armies and Islam penetrates into Central Asia.
767–822 – Dengyo Daishi, founder of the Tendai sect in Japan.
843–45 – new persecutions of the Buddhists in China. The Japanese monk Ennin in China.
1100 approx. – T'ienningsee pagoda in Peking is built.
1133–1212 – Honen Shonin, reformer of the Jodo in Japan.

1197 – the Mohammedans destroy the University of Nalanda.
1206–36 – Mongol invasion of Korea.
1227–63 – Tokiyori favours the Zen movement in Japan. Foundation of the Ikko sect.
1270–94 – revival of Chinese Buddhism under Kublai Khan.
1280–1367 – Yuan era in China; wooden statues.
1340 – Laos converted to Buddhism.
1360 – Buddhism proclaimed the official religion in Siam.
1368–1643 – Ming dynasty in China: extreme refinement and decline of art.
1392–1910 – Yi dynasty in Korea. Confucianism gains a hold. Decline of Buddhism and its art.
1407 – Tsong-kha-pa, Tibetan Buddhist reformer, founds the Gelug-pa sect.
1420–1506 – Sesshu (Zen monk, and painter in ink) and his school in Japan.
1571–7 – Mongol conversion to the Tantric Vehicle. Kum bum monastery founded in Tibet.
1603 – Buddhism begins to decline in Japan.
1642–3 – the fifth Dalai Lama becomes priest-king in Tibet. The Potala is built in Lhasa.
1644–1911 – Ch'ing dynasty: Chinese art continues to decline.
1769 – Shintoism becomes the state religion in Japan.
1891 – establishment of the Maha Bodhi Society.
1906 – establishment of the Buddhist Society of Great Britain.
1909 – Tai-hsu brings about a revival of Buddhism in China.
1929 – establishment of "Les Amis du Bouddhisme" in Paris.
1950 – establishment of the World Fellowship of Buddhists at Colombo, with biennial congresses.
1967 – Tibetan Centre founded in Scotland.

The works reproduced in this book are to be found in the following collections: Karachi, Museum: pp. 6, 7, 12, 13. Kyoto, Korynji monastery: p. 68. Lahore, Central Museum: pp. 27, 29, 33, 34–35, 43. Lhasa, Grand Lamasery: pp. 41, 62. London: Esk Foundation: p. 45; Victoria and Albert Museum: p. 25. Mainamati, Comilla, Archaeological Museum: p. 40. Milan, Eskenazi Collection: p. 52; Poldi and Pezzoli Museum: p. 52. Paris, Bibliothèque Nationale: p. 67; Musée Guimet: pp. 13, 17, 33, 38, 39, 58, 58–9. Peshawar, Museum: pp. 20, 28, 46. Rajshahi Varenda Research Museum: p. 40. Singapore, National Museum: p. 68. Taxila, Archaeological Museum: p. 43. Venice, Marucelliana Library: p. 42. Gabriele Mandel iconographical collection. Photographic references: De Biasi: endpapers, pp. 48, 49, 52, 64, 70. Mandel: pp. 4, 5, 6, 7, 8, 9, 10, 11, 12, 13, 14, 15, 16, 17, 18, 19, 20, 21, 22, 23, 24, 25, 26, 27, 28, 29, 30, 31, 32, 33, 34, 35, 36, 37, 38, 39, 40, 41, 42, 43, 44, 45, 46, 47, 50, 51, 52, 53, 54, 55, 57, 58, 59, 60, 61, 64, 65, 66, 67, 68, 69, 71, 72, 73. Scarnati: pp. 58–9; and Mondadori Photographic Archives.